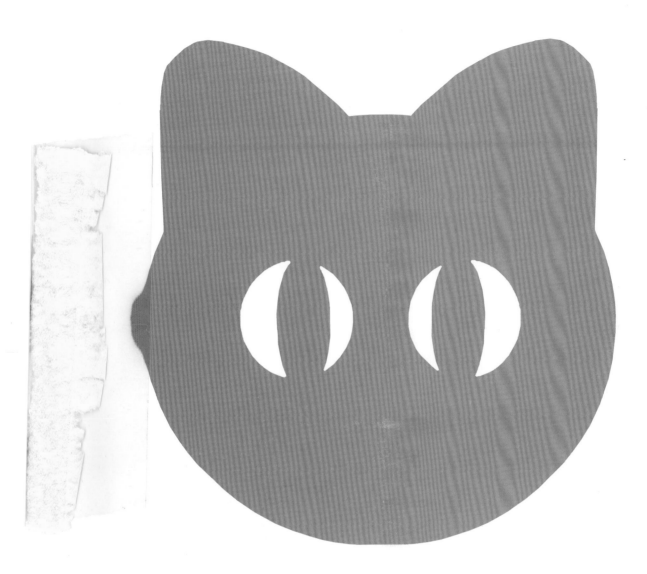

kitty jones kitty crafts

peachbunny

pony

rabbit

slushie

kitty jones
kitty crafts

beautifully designed projects for a cat-friendly home

jen curry

ONE PEACE
BOOKS

Copyright © 2012 by Jen Curry

ISBN: 978-1-935548-21-8

One Peace Books
First Edition: September 2012

Photography © Mark Gore
Photography and illustrations © Jen Curry
Design concept by Nancy Leonard

The projects in this book are intended for personal use of the reader and should be replicated for that purpose only.

Printed in China

Distribution by SCB Distributors
www.scbdistributors.com

For information, contact:
One Peace Books
43-32 22nd Street, Suite #204
Long Island City, NY 11101
www.onepeacebooks.com

This book is dedicated to my amazing
parents, David and Natalie Curry,
whose love for animals and devotion
to family are an inspiration.

contents

introduction

In 2007, my seventeen-year-old cat, Lucy, was experiencing some health issues and much of my focus was devoted to keeping her healthy and happy. I decided to make her a toy. Using some catnip and canvas I found in my studio, I made my first mouse. It was not great-looking—it was huge and the canvas was way too stiff—and was basically unrecognizable as a mouse, so I added all of the defining features, down to the whiskers. I gave it to her anyway and she loved it. It made me so happy to see this side of her again—so playful and lively. Plus the fact that she was getting enjoyment from something that I made was extremely gratifying.

Lucy loved her new toy, but I was on the fence. I was pleased that she was happy, but my first effort was decidedly not cute. The over-accessorized canvas blob just sat there, challenging me. So I set out to make a toy using everything that Lucy liked, but designing it to complement the style choices that were already at play in my life. I pared down the form, taking away features that were unnecessary. The fabrics I chose were more lightweight and special, giving each mouse a recognizable shape and its own personality.

That winter, on a bitterly cold night, I arrived home from a party. I heard a chirping sound in the hallway, and, terrified, made a beeline for my apartment. When I got inside, I kept hearing the sound. I looked through the peephole of my door but saw nothing. My curiosity was piqued, so I opened the door and stepped into the hall. In the corner, I saw a ball of orange fuzz crying for help. I brought him inside and gave him some water and food. I made him a little bed in a box. One of Lucy's mice was on the floor near his bed, and he hopped out and attacked it. He proceeded to hop around the apartment, pouncing on all her toys. He was auditioning for the part of Muse Number 2 and he was killing it. I named him Peachbunny.

Since 2007, I have dedicated myself to all things Cat. I have participated in many markets from New York City to Chicago, and it has been such a pleasure meeting my customers. I have learned so much from all of the conversations, and the knowledge I've gained is reflected in my products. In this book, I have pulled together some of my favorite projects to share with you. My hope is that the projects will not only provide you with well-crafted, personalized items but will also inspire you to learn more about the skills that are utilized to create them. You will find projects in the Play section for your cats to enjoy and projects in the Home section for you to enjoy. No matter which project you choose, each one offers a special way to honor your kitty while enhancing the look of the home that you share.

lucy

peachbunny

getting started

BASIC RULES

ESTABLISH A CLEAN, ORGANIZED SPACE

By establishing a dedicated work area, and laying out your tools in advance, you create an environment that is free of clutter and distraction. Having only the necessary tools at hand enable you to give your full attention to the process.

FAMILIARIZE YOURSELF WITH THE PROJECT

Taking the time to read through the entire project before you begin allows you to see the big picture. Some of these projects are a bit more challenging than others. By gaining a general understanding of the process, and preparing accordingly, you will set yourself up for a rewarding crafting experience.

START SMALL

Each project in this book has been assigned a level of difficulty, indicated by the number of 🐱 (ranging from one, easy, to three, more difficult). If you are new to crafting, I recommend beginning with an easy project—such as the Mouse or Stick in the Play section, or the Bookend or Tray in the Home section—and gradually taking on more challenging projects. By doing this, you will get the lay of the land and gain confidence.

TEMPLATE TIPS

I have provided templates, starting on page 82, for the projects that require them.

COPY OR TRACE TO SIZE

If you choose to follow my dimensions, all of the templates, except for the Friend project* on page 78, are exactly sized for use, so you only need to photocopy or trace them.

*The templates for this project need to be enlarged 200 percent.

STAY PROPORTIONAL

If you choose to make a project to different dimensions, the template should be proportional to these new dimensions, and you will need to minimize or enlarge it.

DO NOT BE AFRAID TO EXPERIMENT

I also encourage you to experiment with using your own images for the projects!

FABRIC PREPARATION TIPS

I prefer to use fabric that is 100-percent cotton, and I would suggest, for best results, that you do the same. For the projects that utilize fabric, the fabric weight and amount needed are indicated in the Materials box. A few of the sewing projects are small enough to put those fabric scraps to good use.

LAUNDER YOUR FABRIC

Fabric should always be laundered before cutting and sewing and/or printing.

Sewing: Whether you choose to machine wash and dry, hand wash, air-dry, or dry clean, you should use the same method when laundering the item after you make it, to prevent shrinkage after the seams are in place. Note: If you are sewing the projects in this book by hand, I recommend hand-washing only, to insure that the integrity of your craft remains intact.

Printing: Manufacturers put starch and other conditioners into fabric to enable the material to stay wrinkle-free, and these additives may inhibit the absorption of ink. For more information on printing fabric, see page 73.

PRESS YOUR FABRIC

After laundering and before cutting, carefully iron your fabric, using the proper heat-setting. Not only can working with wrinkled fabric be frustrating, but the size of your sewing project may be off when completed. For printing, you want your surface to be as smooth as possible for best results.

SEWING TIPS

KNOW YOUR FABRIC SIDES

The "right side" of the fabric is visible when the project is finished; the "wrong side" of the fabric is unseen on a finished project.

BACKSTITCH OR REVERSE STITCH

When sewing by hand or machine, always use a backstitch or reverse stitch, to lock the stitch in place and prevent unraveling.

Hand sewing: Place the fabric pieces together and pass the needle through the layers. Pass the needle back through the layers, ⅛" (3 mm) to the right of where you started, then to the left, back over the starting point by ⅛" (3 mm) and through. Repeat until the entire opening is sewn closed.

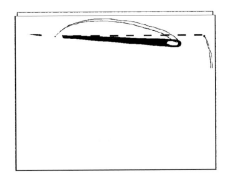

Machine sewing: When starting a seam, place your machine's needle ¼" (6 mm) below your starting point. Use the reverse stitch function on your machine until you reach the starting point, then begin stitching forward. When finishing a seam, carry your forward stitch to the end point, then use the reverse stitch function to go back over the stitches ¼" (6 mm).

PIVOT AT THE CORNERS (sewing machine only)

For the sewing projects that are rectangular in shape, you are encouraged to sew a continuous seam rather than individual seams for each side, which means pivoting at the corners. When you reach a corner, lift the presser foot, while keeping the needle in the fabric, and turn your project, then put your presser foot back down and continue sewing.

play

Cats love to play. Whether it is with you or on their own, there's no denying that your cat's (second) best friend is his or her favorite toy. I have compiled several of Peachbunny's favorite playthings and accessories in this section. All of these projects utilize the same elements that I have used to define the style of kitty jones: simplified form, quality materials, and a keen focus on fulfilling the desires of my feline friend. Have fun and personalize each item to suit your needs, as well as the needs of your cat.

mouse

- ¼ yd (23 cm) lightweight fabric
- Mouse template, page 82
- Paper
- Ruler
- Fabric shears
- Pins
- Tailor's pencil or chalk
- Hand-sewing needle
- Thread
- Sewing maching (optional)
- Point turner
- Fill
- 1 tbsp (15 ml) dried catnip
- 4" (10 cm) long jute cord

Kitty jones started with a catnip mouse. The first recipient was my 18-year-old cat, Lucy, and she loved it…so much, in fact, that my friend Jen said, "You should sell those things!" This version is simplified and smaller. It is a fun toy for a cat who likes to fetch, as well as for those sensitive types who love a good cuddle. Adjust the amount of catnip to your liking—use a bit for a mellow experience or a lot if you really want to blow your kitty's mind.

difficulty:

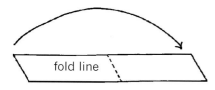

fold line

step 4

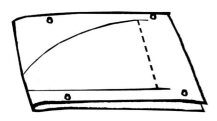

step 5

1. Prepare fabric by laundering and pressing.

2. Copy or trace the template provided on page 82 and cut out.

3. Measure and cut a 3" x 6" (7.5 x 15 cm) piece of fabric

4. Fold the fabric in half lengthwise, right sides together, and pin *(see illustration)*.

5. Position the template on the fabric, with the small end of the template on the fold line, and trace the solid lines with the tailor's pencil *(see illustration)*. Note: The dotted line indicates an area to be left unsewn. Remove template.

6. Using either needle and thread or a sewing machine, sew along the two traced lines, starting at the fabric fold.

7. Trim the fabric ¼" (6 mm) from the seams. Note: Do not trim the excess fabric at the open end.

8. Invert the sewn fabric by running the point turner along the inside seams of the fabric, to encourage the fabric to invert and to push out the tip. Fold the excess fabric at the open end inside the body to meet the fill.

9. Sprinkle fill with the catnip, then stuff the mouse, using the point turner to encourage the fill into the body until it is sufficiently full.

10. Tie a knot at each end of the piece of jute cord. Place one of the knotted ends inside the open end of the mouse.

11. Hand-sew the opening closed, paying close attention to the area around the knot in order to secure the tail. Tie the thread off.

what else?

Using thin leather cord for the tail instead of jute will take your mouse from the country to the city.

grass

- Clear jar or empty can (coffee, soup, etc.)
- Small garden stones
- Charcoal
- Potting soil
- 1 packet grass seeds (wheat grass or rye)
- Water
- Plastic wrap

Additional for can planter

- Hammer
- Nail
- Straight-edge ruler
- Pencil
- Decorative paper
- Scissors
- Craft glue
- Paper clip

I live in New York City, so Peachbunny is an indoor guy, except when we visit my parents in Pennsylvania—then he's a porch guy. I imagine he dreams of lazing in the warm summer sun, delighting in the brightness of fresh grass as it passes over his palate. While I always knew he would enjoy some fresh grass of his own, I could never get past the plastic containers included with grass kits sold at pet stores. These grass planters solve that issue, offering something for everyone. They bring a bit of the outside in, aid our little buddies with digestion, and, depending on which design you choose, either provide a beautiful lesson in irrigation or inject a bit of pattern into your décor.

difficulty:

JAR PLANTER

1. Fill the jar with garden stones to just below the halfway mark and cover with a solid layer of charcoal.

2. Fill the jar with potting soil to just below the rim.

3. For wheat grass: sprinkle seeds on top of potting soil, water, and cover with plastic wrap. For rye: sprinkle seeds on top of potting soil, cover with a light layer of potting soil, water, and cover with plastic wrap. Note: Follow the directions on the seed packet for the amount of seeds to plant.

4. Place in a sunny window for a few days until the seeds begin to sprout, then remove plastic wrap and check the soil to make sure it isn't dry. If dry, lightly water. Allow grass to grow at least 3" (7.5 cm) before presenting to your cat.

5. Keep the grass trimmed, to approximately 3" (7.5 cm) and water regularly.

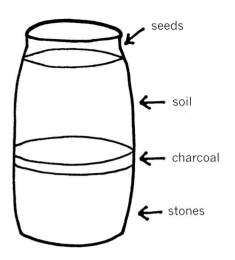

seeds
soil
charcoal
stones

what else?

In place of paper, consider using fabric-wrapped cardstock for the can decoration. Once you figure the cardstock's dimensions (see steps 8–10, page 22), refer to the Bookend project (steps 8–12, page 59) for fabric application.

CAN PLANTER

Add the decorative paper to this planter after the grass has grown.

1. Clean and thoroughly dry can.

2. Use a hammer and nail to punch a series of holes in the bottom of the can for drainage. Note: When completed, you may want to place your can planter on a plate or tray to catch excess water.

3. Fill the can with a spare layer of stones and cover with a solid layer of charcoal.

4. Fill the can with potting soil to just below the rim.

5. For wheat grass: sprinkle seeds on top of potting soil, water, and cover with plastic wrap. For rye: sprinkle seeds on top of potting soil, cover with a light layer of potting soil, water, and cover with plastic wrap. Note: Follow the directions on the seed packet for the amount of seeds to plant.

6. Place in a sunny window for a few days until the seeds begin to sprout, then remove plastic wrap and check the soil to make sure it isn't dry. If dry, lightly water. Allow grass to grow at least 3" (7.5 cm) before presenting to your cat.

7. Keep the grass trimmed, to approximately 3" (7.5 cm) and water regularly.

8. For the can's decoration: Measure the height and circumference of the can (see illustration). Note: To calculate the circumference, measure the diameter, from one side of the can to the other across its center point, then multiply that number by 3.1416. Add ½" (13 mm) to the circumference.

9. Using the dimensions from step 8, a pencil, and a straight-edge ruler, draw a rectangle on the back of a sheet of decorative paper (see illustration).

10. Cut the paper and wrap around the can. Overlap the edges, gluing the paper to itself. Secure with a paper clip until dry.

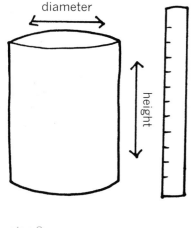

step 8

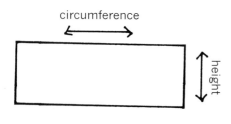

step 9

stick

Do not be fooled by the simple shape of this cat toy. From the feedback I have received from many of my customers, this stick is a feline favorite—there is no denying that almost every cat loves a good old kicking stick. Now you can make a custom stick for your cat, using some of your favorite fabric.

difficulty:

1. Prepare fabric by laundering and pressing.

2. Measure and cut a 3" x 13" (7.5 x 33 cm) piece of fabric.

3. Fold the fabric in half lengthwise, right sides facing together, and pin *(see illustration)*.

4. Using either needle and thread or a sewing machine, sew the entire length of the two long sides, ¼" (6 mm) from the fabric edge. Leave the short end open.

5. Invert the sewn fabric by running the point turner along the inside seams of the fabric to encourage the fabric to invert and to push out the corners.

6. Sprinkle fill with the catnip, then stuff the stick, using the point turner to encourage the fill into the fabric until it is sufficiently full.

7. Tuck in the fabric of the open end 1" (2.5 cm) to make a clean edge *(see illustration)*. Hand-sew the opening closed. Tie the thread off.

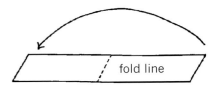

fold line

step 3

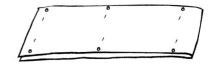

what else?

If your cat is a more of a lounger, adding some length to your fabric will take your stick from a kicker to a cuddler.

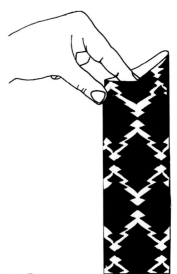

step 7

bed

materials

- ½ yd (46 cm) 54" (137 cm) medium- to heavyweight fabric
- Ruler
- Fabric shears
- Iron
- Pins
- ⅝" (16 mm) or ¾" (2 cm) thick sewable Velcro strip, at least 24" (61 cm) long
- Thread
- Sewing machine
- ½ yd (46 cm) 1" (2.5 cm) thick foam
- ½ yd (46 cm) 48" (122 cm) batting

Animals love a designated spot they can call their own. I take Peachbunny with me to my parents' house a few times a year and always bring along a pet bed to insure his comfort. He really loves his bed, and, to be completely honest, he has several. He's spoiled, yes, but it isn't hard when the project can be made with ease. This bed is a simple design that travels well and looks great at home. The cover is removable so washing is a breeze, and the flat shape allows him to sit comfortably or sprawl after a playdate with the Mouse (page 16).

difficulty:

step 3

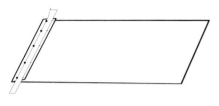

step 4

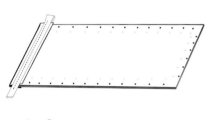

step 6

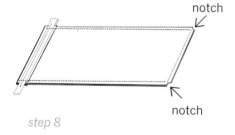

notch

notch

step 8

1. Prepare fabric by laundering and pressing.

2. Measure and cut two 16" x 22" (40.5 x 56 cm) pieces of fabric.

3. Create a 1" (2.5 cm) fold on one of the short sides of one of the pieces of fabric, right side folded toward the wrong side *(see illustration)*. Pin to secure (optional). Iron fold to create a crisp edge, removing pins as you go. Repeat on the second piece of fabric.

4. Separate the Velcro strip into two strips. Pin one of the strips along the folded fabric of one of the pieces, ¼" (6 mm) from the folded edge *(see illustration)*. Note: Pin the Velcro and fabric at the same time. Repeat with the second Velcro strip and fabric piece. Note: Your Velcro strips will extend beyond the fabric.

5. Using a matching thread color to your fabric, sew the Velcro strips to each piece of fabric, sewing a line down the center, along the entire length of the Velcro.

6. Place the fabric pieces, right sides together, making sure to align the Velcro strips. Note: The Velcro will be on the outside of the case at this point. Pin three sides, leaving the Velcro edge unpinned *(see illustration)*.

7. Begin sewing on one of the long sides, at the fabric fold. Note: You will stitch over the Velcro strip. Stitch the three pinned sides, ¼" (6 mm) from the fabric edge, pivoting at the corners and ending the seam on the opposite long side of the fabric.

8. Before inverting the fabric, cut a notch at each of the corners *(see illustration)*. Be careful not to clip the seam. Note: Notching the fabric in this way will encourage the shape of the corners when the fabric is inverted in the next step. Trim the excess length of the Velcro strips to the fabric edge.

9. Invert the fabric, and, with your hand, push gently along the seams, to encourage the rectangular form.

10. Cut a 14" x 20" (35 x 51 cm) piece of foam.

11. Cut a 14" x 44" (35 x 112 cm) piece of batting and wrap neatly around the foam.

12. Insert the foam cushion and Velcro shut.

what else?

You can make a simple case for the foam insert by folding a piece of muslin (you will need ½ yd, or 46 cm) over the cushion lengthwise and sewing the two long sides closed.

ball

materials

Needle felting

- 1 to 2 ounces wool roving, depending on size of ball
- Needle-felting tool
- Foam pad

Wet felting

- 1 to 2 ounces wool roving, depending on size of ball
- Sink or basin
- ¼ cup (60 ml) unscented liquid soap
- 6 cups (1.4 l) hot water

A couple of years ago, my friend Alyson invited me to join her for a needle-felting class. I had never felted anything before but was intrigued by the beauty and sustainability of the material. The first thing our instructor taught us was how to make a wool ball. I found the process to be meditative and addictive. When I finished the first ball, I bounced it and thought, This would be great for cats. And it is. Not only are the balls bouncy and lightweight—making them easy to bat around and carry—cats are drawn to the natural scent of the wool. Here I share two felting methods: needle felting and wet felting. Your cat will love the result of either method you choose!

difficulty:

NEEDLE FELTING

Needle felting uses a barbed needle tool to push and pull the strands of roving to create a knit. The more you poke the layers with the needle, the denser the knit becomes. Use the needle slowly, being mindful of your fingers and thumb.

1. Peel a long, narrow sliver (approximately ¼", or 6 mm, wide) of roving *(see illustration)*. Note: Never use scissors to cut roving. To select a small length of roving, simply choose the amount you would like to work with and pull apart lengthwise. Using your thumb and forefinger, squeeze and roll the end together to form a bead *(see illustration)*.

2. Slowly turn the bead so that the roving wraps around it. The roving needs to be quite thin at this point. Turn the bead as you go so the strands crisscross.

3. Once you've made 3 to 4 passes over the bead, place it on the foam pad with the roving still intact. Note: The foam pad is necessary for two reasons: it protects the surface that you are working on and creates a buffer for the delicate tip of the needle. Using the felting needle, poke the bead several times, turning it over to address every side.

4. Continue to wrap with the roving, making sure to cover the bead consistently. Use your thumb and forefinger to compress the roving, and the needle to lock the strands into place *(see illustration)*. As the ball grows, some areas may require more attention with the needle. Note: This is the meditative part—take your time crafting the ball.

5. Continue to wrap and poke. Depending on the desired size, when you reach the end of the original strand of roving, you may either finish by securing the final strands with the needle or continue with another piece of roving. To continue, pull another thin sliver of roving, use the felting needle to secure the end to the ball, and repeat step 4.

step 1a

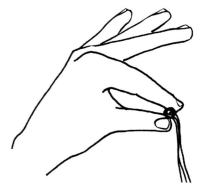

step 1b

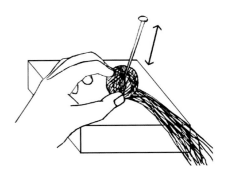

step 4

what else?

With play, wools balls can gather dirt and the fibers may begin to loosen. To remedy this, just toss the ball into a load of laundry (be careful to wash brightly colored balls separately!), then into the dryer to re-felt.

step 1a

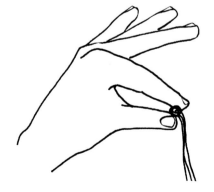

step 1b

WET FELTING

Wet felting uses hot water and soap to shrink the roving's fibers. It is less time-consuming than needle felting, resulting in a ball that is more cushiony and less dense than the needle-felted variety.

1. Peel a long, narrow sliver (approximately ¼", or 6 mm, wide) of roving *(see illustration)*. Note: Never use scissors to cut roving. To select a small length of roving, simply choose the amount you would like to work with and pull apart lengthwise. Using your thumb and forefinger, squeeze and roll the end together to form a bead *(see illustration)*.

2. Slowly turn the bead so that the roving wraps around it. The roving needs to be quite thin at this point. Turn the bead as you go so the strands crisscross. Keep wrapping in this fashion until you have created a ball that is twice as large as your desired size. Note: For a bigger ball, you will need to add more roving.

3. Using a sink or basin, dissolve the liquid detergent in the hot water. The hotter the water, the better, but adjust to your comfort and be sure to test before fully submerging your hands. Note: Using unscented soap will retain the natural fragrance of the wool.

4. Submerge the ball into the hot, soapy liquid. Remove from the liquid and roll the ball between your palms to encourage the ball shape. Note: The ball will be drippy so stand over the sink or basin. When the ball begins to cool, submerge it into the soapy water again.

5. Continue rolling and submerging until the ball has shrunk to desired size. Give it a final rinse with cool water to remove excess soap and allow to air-dry.

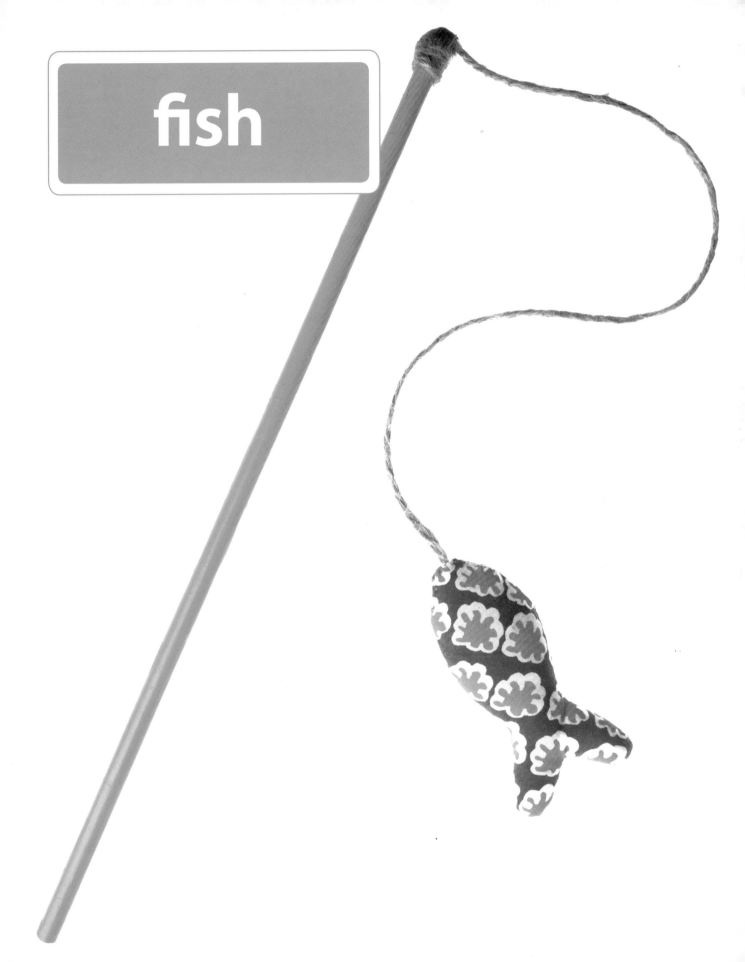

fish

materials

- ¼ yd (23 cm) lightweight fabric
- Fish template, page 82
- Paper
- ½" (13 mm) thick dowel rod, at least 18" (45.5 cm) long
- Fine grain sand paper (optional)
- Acrylic craft paint (optional)
- Water-based polyurethane (optional)
- 24" (61 cm) jute cord
- Ruler
- Fabric shears
- Pins
- Tailor's pencil or chalk
- Hand-sewing needle
- Thread
- Sewing machine (optional)
- Fill
- 1 tbsp (15 ml) dried catnip
- Point turner
- Hot glue gun

Everyone knows that one of the easiest ways to play with a cat is with a toy that moves. This fishing pole is a fun toy for cats, adults, and children alike. Cats love the attention they get when people play with them, and they get a little exercise, too. Now you can play with your cat in a stylish way. Choose a cute fabric for the fish and paint the rod a vibrant, contrasting color.

difficulty:

1. Prepare fabric by laundering and pressing. Set aside.

2. Copy or trace the template provided on page 82 and cut out. Set aside.

3. Cut the dowel rod to 18" (45.5 cm). Lightly sand the edges, if desired.

4. (Optional step) Paint the rod using acrylic craft paint: Starting in the center of the rod, paint in one direction, all the way to the end, including the tip. Prop the painted edge so it can dry. When dry, repeat this step from the center to the opposite end. Allow to dry. Once the paint has dried, add a protective finish, using the water-based polyurethane, and allow to dry.

5. Knot one end of the jute cord, leaving a ¼" (6 mm) tail *(see illustration)*. Set aside.

step 5

6. Measure and cut two 4" x 5" (10 x 12.5 cm) pieces of fabric and place right sides together. Pin.

7. Place the template on top of the fabric pieces. Using the tailor's pencil, trace the solid line of the template onto the fabric. Note: The dotted line indicates an area to be left unsewn. Remove the template.

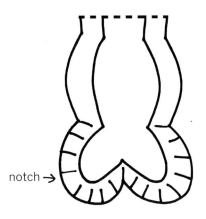

notch →

8. Using either needle and thread or a sewing machine, begin sewing at the mouth of the fish, along the traced line. Follow the line around the entire fish.

step 9

9. Trim the fabric ¼" (6 mm) from the seam. Leave ½" (13 mm) of extra fabric at the open end. Snip the areas where the seam curves, at a perpendicular angle to the seam *(see illustration)*. Be careful not to clip the seam. Note: Notching the fabric in this way will encourage the shape of the curves when the fabric is inverted in the next step

10. Invert the sewn fabric by running the point turner along the inside seam of the fabric to encourage the fabric to invert and to push out the curves. Once inverted, tuck the excess fabric at the mouth into the body to create a straight line *(see illustration)*.

11. Sprinkle fill with the catnip, then stuff the fish, using the point turner to encourage the fill into the body until it is sufficiently full.

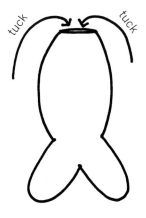

tuck   tuck

what else?

To really get your cat's attention when playing together, insert a jingle bell (about ½", or 13 mm, in size) when stuffing the fish.

step 10

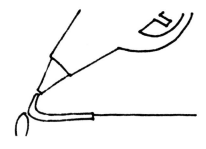

step 14a

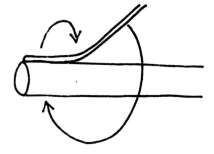

step 14b

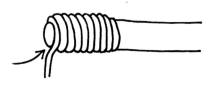

step 14c

12. Place the knotted end of the jute cord in the fish mouth. Hand-sew the opening closed, taking care to secure the knot inside the fish. Tie the thread off.

13. Wrap the other end of the jute cord around one end of the rod a few times to make sure that you are happy with the length of the cord. Trim if necessary.

14. Beginning at one end, draw a 1" (2.5 cm) bead of hot glue down the rod *(see illustration)*. Align the end of the jute cord with the end of the rod and affix along the bead. Wrap the jute around the rod, back toward the tip, encasing the already glued edge of the cord *(see illustration)*. When you reach the end of the rod, place a final bead of hot glue on the tip and hold until secure *(see illustration)*.

scratch pad

materials

- 2 yds (1.8 m) grosgrain ribbon
- Straight-edge ruler
- Pencil
- 1 to 2 cardboard boxes (see step 2, opposite, for dimensions), depending on size of scratch pad
- X-acto knife
- Self-healing mat
- Flat paintbrush
- Craft glue
- Pinking shears

My cat loves to scratch my furniture. Whose doesn't? And he always seems to go for the one piece that I love the most. One afternoon, while I was breaking down cardboard boxes for recycling, and as Peachbunny went to work on a formerly pristine mid-century chair, it dawned on me: I should make him a cat scratcher. But how was I going to make the cardboard boxes attractive? I liked the idea of a bold graphic, so I wrapped my scratch pad with colorful grosgrain ribbon.

difficulty:

1. Measure the width of your ribbon. This measurement will determine the width of your cardboard strips, which will also be the height of your scratch pad. Note: Grosgrain ribbon comes in many different widths so if you would like a scratcher that lies close to the floor, choose a narrow width; for a taller scratcher, choose a wider width. My shorter scratch pad has a ribbon width of 1¾" (4.5 cm); and the taller one has a ribbon width of 3½" (9 cm).

2. Choose a box with dimensions in which the shorter side can accommodate the length you want your scratch pad to be. Note: My scratch pads are 18" (45 cm) long. Remove the flaps of the box and cut along the four vertical folds so you are left with twelve flat, uninterrupted pieces. Look carefully at the sides of one of the pieces of cardboard, taking note of the direction of the corrugation. Note: You will cut the cardboard in a perpendicular direction to the corrugated line (see illustration).

3. If your cardboard pieces are longer than the desired length of your scratch pad, use your X-acto knife to cut the pieces to the correct length.

4. Decide how wide you want your scratch pad to be. Note: My scratch pads are 10" (25.5 cm) wide. Now measure the thickness of your cardboard, then figure out how many strips of cardboard per inch (cm) you will need. Note: My cardboard is ⅙" (4 mm) thick, which equals 6 strips of cardboard per inch (2.5 cm).

5. Multiply the width of your scratch pad by the number of cardboard strips per inch (cm). This will give you the total number of strips you need to cut. Note: I multiplied 10" (25.5 cm) by 6 (my number of strips per inch, or 2.5 cm, based on the cardboard's thickness). I cut 60 strips for each of my scratch pads.

6. Using the straight-edge ruler, mark the edge of the cardboard in increments that correspond to the width of the ribbon. Repeat on the opposite edge (see illustration). Note: You may need to use multiple cardboard pieces, depending on your ribbon width and the number of strips you calculated in step 4.

7. Place the cardboard on a self-healing mat. Line up your straight-edge ruler between the corresponding marks on the cardboard and use the X-acto knife to cut from one edge to the other. Continue cutting until you amass the desired number of strips.

8. Apply a stream of glue to one side of a cardboard strip (see illustration). Stand it horizontally, on a flat surface, and align another strip to it, making sure the ends of the strips are flush. Press to secure. Apply a stream of glue to the second strip and press a third strip against it. Repeat until all the strips are glued in place.

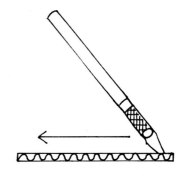

step 2

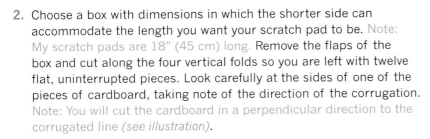

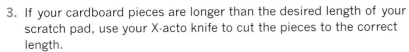

step 6

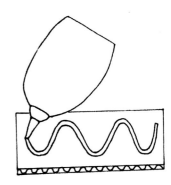

step 8

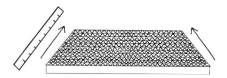

step 9

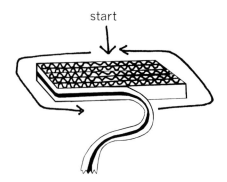

start

step 11

9. Measure the length of the short end of the scratcher *(see illustration)*. Cut two pieces of cardboard to that length and the width of your cardboard strips (aka your ribbon width), and glue to the short ends, creating a smooth edge. Allow to dry.

10. Figure out the circumference of the scratch pad by adding its length and width and multiplying that number by 2. Add 2" (5 cm) to the circumference, and cut your ribbon to this length. Note: I cut a 58" (1.5 m) length of ribbon for each of my scratchers.

11. Starting at the center of one of the long sides, use a paintbrush to apply a consistent 3" (7.5 cm) length of glue. Position the ribbon on top of the glue and hold until secure. Continue to apply the glue with the paintbrush, affixing the ribbon as you go, until the entire scratcher is wrapped *(see illustration)*. Before gluing the overlapping ribbon, use pinking shears to cut the ribbon end so it doesn't fray. Note: If you don't have pinking shears, apply a thin stream of glue to the underside of the ribbon, fold under, and hold until secure.

what else?

If you would like a tall scratcher but cannot find a wide ribbon that accommodates your design, consider layering more than one ribbon.

star

materials

- 8½" x 14" (21.5 x 35.5 cm), aka legal size, copy paper
- Straight-edge ruler
- Pencil
- Scissors or X-acto knife
- Self-healing mat (optional)

Peachbunny loves a good old-fashioned paper ball. It is almost weightless, making it a perfect toy to bat around and carry. I wanted to make a toy that we could mutually appreciate—something pretty and simple, rather than something that looked like it missed the wastebasket. Origami, an intricate method of folding paper, is a Japanese art form that produces elegant paper sculptures. The results can be simple or complex, but they are always sophisticated. These stars are lightweight and small enough for Peachbunny to carry in his mouth, and they are light-years more interesting and beautiful than a crumpled paper ball.

difficulty:

1. Measure and cut the paper into a 1" x 14" (2.5 x 36 cm) strip.

2. Starting at one end of the strip, wrap 3½" (9 cm) of the paper around your index finger *(see illustration)*. Note: If the paper is two-tone, the color you desire for the star should be facing you.

3. Make a loop with the paper and tuck the end inside the loop *(see illustration)*.

4. Carefully tighten to create a flat knot *(see illustration)*.

5. Turn the knot over and fold the short end toward the center of the knot, tucking it in and creating a crisp crease at the fold *(see illustration)*. Your paper should look like a flat pentagon at this stage *(see illustration)*.

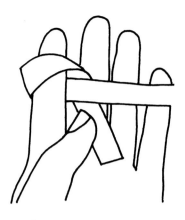

step 2

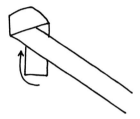

step 3

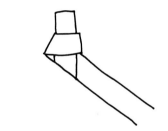

step 4

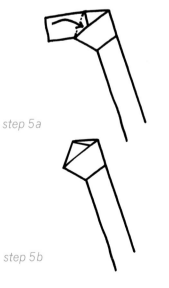

step 5a

step 5b

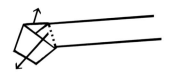

step 6a

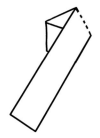

step 6b

tuck

step 7

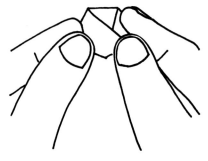

step 8

6. Fold the long end up and to the left, aligning the edges of the paper with the edges of the pentagon *(see illustration)*. Continue folding, using the pentagon edges as your guides *(see illustration)*.

7. Once you have reached the end of the strip, tuck the end into the body of the pentagon *(see illustration)*.

8. Once the end is neatly tucked in, use the nails on your thumbs and forefingers to "inflate" the star *(see illustration)*. Push on the center point of each side to create a dent. Rotate and continue applying pressure until the star shape emerge.

completed star

what else?

Legend has it that origami stars are lucky. Fold several and keep them in a jar for good fortune.

scratch post

materials

- 18" (45.5 cm) tall heavy-duty cardboard tube or PVC pipe
- Flat piece of cardboard
- Pencil
- Wooden disc, approximately 15" (38 cm) in diameter
- Hot glue gun
- ¼" (6 mm) thick sisal rope, at least 100 ft (30.5 m) long

Cats love to scratch. Walk into any pet store and you are bound to find a selection of vertical scratchers. These offerings are often imposing and made with carpet remnants. To me, the most attractive functional pieces are the ones designed with a streamlined approach, balancing utility with the elegance of a natural material. This scratch post accomplishes that while benefiting from the added bonus of a recycled carpet tube. So the carpet does belong in this design… just not in the expected way.

difficulty:

1. Place the cardboard tube so that the end is perpendicular to the flat piece of cardboard. Trace the circumference of the tube. Cut the cardboard, along the traced line. Set aside the circular cutout.

2. Measure the center point of the wooden disc and mark with an X.

3. Find the diameter of the cardboard tube by measuring from one side to the other across its center point. Divide the diameter by 2. Use this number to make four equidistant marks from the X on the disc (see illustration).

4. Stand the cardboard tube on the wooden disc, using the marks as your guide, so it's directly in the center. Trace the circumference of the tube with the pencil.

5. Apply a line of hot glue along the drawn circumference line on the wooden disc. Adhere the cardboard tube, applying moderate pressure and holding in place until the glue is set. Note: Work quickly, as hot glue cools rapidly.

6. Apply a line of hot glue around the top edge of the tube and adhere the cardboard cutout you set aside in step 1 to cap the tube (see illustration).

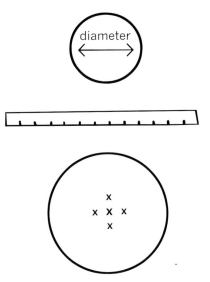

step 3

step 6

what else?

For a softer feel, use cotton rope, such as that used for a clothesline. Remember to stay with natural materials since you will be using hot glue, and synthetic materials, like nylon, can melt under high heat.

7. To adhere the sisal rope, begin by applying a 3" (7.5 cm) length of glue along the bottom edge of the wooden base. Attach the rope to the glue and hold until secure. Repeat.

8. Continue to glue, wrapping the rope around the circumference of the wooden base and along the top of it, in concentric circles, until you reach the bottom of the cardboard tube *(see illustration)*.

9. When you reach the cardboard tube, continue gluing and wrapping the rope as closely as possible to the base of the tube, then begin climbing the tube.

10. When you reach the top of the tube, wrap the rope around the perimeter so it rests a little higher than the cap. Note: This will create a consistent boundary for the rope that covers the top of the tube, providing a clean silhouette. Continue wrapping toward the center of the top of the tube *(see illustration)*.

11. Before applying the last bit of glue in the center, tuck the rope into the remaining space on the cardboard cap. Take note of the end point on the remaining length of rope, untuck, and cut. Finish with one last length of glue, tucking the end of the rope and its fray into the glue. Note: Hold the rope end in place with the pencil or other object to prevent your hand from having direct contact with the hot glue.

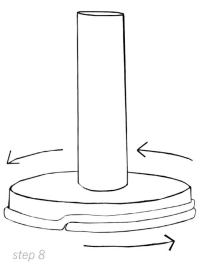

step 8

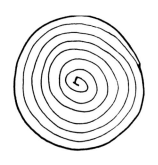

step 10

house

materials

- House templates, page 83
- Paper
- 2 new 18"(l) x 14"(w) x 12"(h) cardboard boxes (45.5 x 35.5 x 30.5 cm)
- X-acto knife
- Self-healing mat
- Pencil
- Paper tape
- Hot glue gun
- up to 4 colors construction paper, archival preferred (see What Else?, page 52)
- Scissors
- Craft glue

Peachbunny loves a cardboard box. There is an unmistakable glint in his eye when he hears the UPS truck idling outside my apartment building. While I am certainly willing to go to great lengths to make my buddy happy, keeping a non-descript cardboard box around for his amusement doesn't quite fit my design scheme. This house is a great way to satisfy your kitty's love for a cardboard box while meeting your standards for a well-appointed home.

difficulty:

HOUSE

1. Copy or trace the templates on page 83 and cut out.

2. Cut along one of the vertical folds of one of the boxes, using the X-acto knife on a self-healing mat, to create a long, flat piece *(see illustration)*.

3. Position the door and window templates on the box as desired. Note: Include at least five windows, as you will use the door and window remnants later. Trace templates onto box, then cut out with the X-acto knife *(see illustration)*. Set door and window remnants aside.

4. On the inside of one of the top short flaps, measure the top center point. Draw two lines from this point to the bottom corners of the flap. Repeat on the opposite top short flap *(see illustration)*.

5. Score the two lines on each of the flaps with the X-acto knife *(see illustration)*. Note: Do not cut through the flaps.

6. Tape the vertical fold that you cut in step 2 with paper tape. Assemble box by folding in the bottom flaps. Leave top flaps open.

7. Fold each of the top long flaps toward the center of the box. Fold and hot glue the four scored triangles of the short flaps to the long flaps *(see illustration)*.

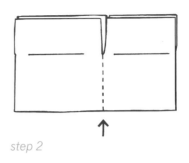

step 2

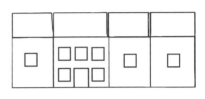

step 3

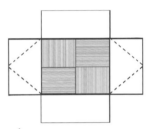

step 4

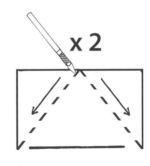

step 5

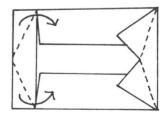

step 7

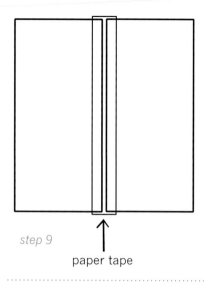

step 9

paper tape

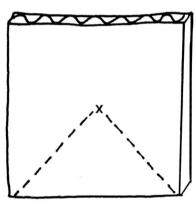

step 13

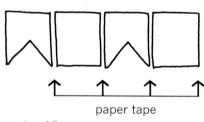

paper tape

step 16

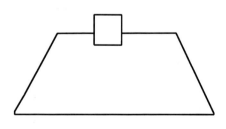

step 17

ROOF

8. Remove the two long sides of the second box with the X-acto knife.

9. Align the two sides with $^3/_8$" (10 mm) between them, then connect with a piece of paper tape along the entire length of the sides *(see illustration)*.

10. Center the roof on top of the house.

11. While holding in place, gently lift one side of the roof and apply hot glue to the house structure beneath. Apply light pressure until secure. Repeat with the opposite side of the roof and house.

CHIMNEY

12. Measure the center point of one of the window remnants and mark with an X.

13. Draw two lines, beginning at the X and extending to the bottom corners *(see illustration)*.

14. Use the X-acto knife to cut along the lines, removing the trianguluar cutout from the remnant.

15. Repeat steps 12–14 on a second window remnant.

16. Lay the two angled pieces on a flat surface. Place a full window remnant between each of the angled pieces, leaving $^3/_8$" (10 mm) between each piece. Using three strips of paper tape, connect the pieces. Complete the chimney by connecting the first and last pieces with a fourth piece of paper tape *(see illustration)*.

17. Place chimney on roof in desired location *(see illustration)*. Secure with ½" (6 mm) wide strips of paper tape along the sides of the chimney that meet the roof.

what else?

Choose fewer colors of construction paper for a minimal design scheme. Archival construction paper is preferred as it's less prone to fading.

DECORATION

18. For the house and roof: Use the shingle template to cut shingles out of construction paper. Note: For a scalloped edge, round the bottom corners of the shingle with your scissors. Starting at the bottom of each section, attach shingles, with craft glue, in a tiled format *(see illustration)*. Note: The total number of shingles needed depends on how closely you place them.

19. For the chimney: Use the chimney brick template to cut bricks out of construction paper. Starting at the top of the chimney, attach bricks, with craft glue, in a tiled format, leaving space between each brick to create a mortar effect *(see illustration)*.

20. For the window and door frames: Trace the remaining window and door remnants to create the inner part of the frames. For the outer part of the frames, measure and draw a rectangle ¾" (2 cm) outside of each of the traced inner frames. Cut along the lines of the inner and outer frames and use craft glue to place around door and windows.

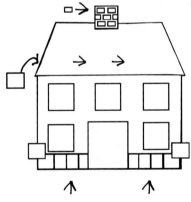

steps 18–19

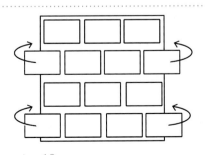

step 19

home

With the pared-down approach I used for the Play projects, I saw an opportunity to honor my kitty in a subtle, decorative way. The projects in this section are inspired by my love for cats—some are useful and others are purely ornamental. The classic form of each project lends itself nicely to customization, allowing your personal style to shine.

bookend

materials

- ¼ yd (23 cm) lightweight fabric
- Bookend template, page 84, or your own image
- Paper
- Pair of 5" (12.5 cm) tall metal bookends
- Flat piece of cardboard
- Pencil
- X-acto knife
- Self-healing mat
- Ruler
- Fabric shears
- Tailor's pencil or chalk
- Craft glue
- Flat paintbrush

You can tell so much about a person by the books they display on a shelf. A fun way to add a bit more of your personality to a collection of books is by creating a pair of custom bookends that show off the silhouette of your beloved kitty. Have fun with mixing your fabric patterns and colors for a perfectly mismatched set.

difficulty:

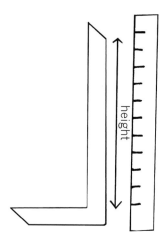

step 2

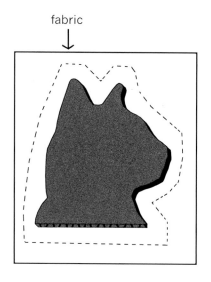

fabric

step 6

1. Prepare fabric by laundering and pressing. Set aside.

2. If using the template provided on page 84, copy or trace it, resize if necessary, and cut out. If using your own image, enlarge or minimize it, print, and cut out. If your image doesn't have a flat edge at the bottom, create a flat edge. Note: If your bookends are a different height than the ones I used, measure the height of one of the bookends, then size the height of your silhouette to eclipse the bookend's edge *(see illustration)*.

3. Trace two silhouettes onto a piece of cardboard, leaving a little room between them. Remove the template. Use the X-acto knife on a self-healing mat to cut the shape of one of the silhouettes, following the traced line. Repeat for the second silhouette.

4. If using the template and following my dimensions, cut two 9" x 9" (23 x 23 cm) pieces of fabric. If using your own image or different dimensions, make sure there is at least 1" (2.5 cm) of extra fabric around the cardboard silhouette in the next step.

5. Lay the first cardboard silhouette on the wrong side of one of the pieces of fabric, taking notice of placement. Note: Some fabric patterns don't require special placement, but others, such as geometric prints, may require a bit more consideration. Trace around the cardboard silhouette, using the tailor's pencil.

6. Trim the fabric ¾" (2 cm) from the cardboard, mimicking the shape of the silhouette *(see illustration)*.

7. Repeat steps 5–6 for the second silhouette. Make sure to orient the silhouette in the opposite direction so the bookends will either face away from each other or toward each other on the shelf.

what else?

Decorative paper is also an option. Follow steps 8–10 (opposite), then use an X-acto knife on a self-healing mat to trim the excess paper around the cardboard silhouette.

8. Using glue and the paintbrush, apply an even coat of glue to the front of one of the cardboard silhouettes.

9. Place the glue-covered silhouette on the wrong side of the fabric. Note: Use the traced line from step 5 as your guide, in order to have an even amount of extra fabric remaining around the perimeter. Apply pressure to the silhouette and flip over.

10. Using clean hands, smooth the fabric over the cardboard, encouraging air bubbles out toward the edge. Allow to dry.

11. Using your X-acto knife, make small cuts ¼" (6 mm) apart in the fabric, cutting from the edge of the cardboard out to the fabric edge, around the entire perimeter of the silhouette (see illustration). Note: Begin the cut as close to the cardboard as possible without actually meeting the edge.

12. Using the paintbrush, apply glue to the back of the cardboard silhouette, within 1" (2.5 cm) of the outside edge only. Begin folding the fabric around the edge of the silhouette, overlapping it as you go and holding it in place to secure the fabric to the cardboard (see illustration). Allow to dry.

13. Repeat steps 8–12 with the second silhouette.

14. Apply a bead of glue along the length of the vertical edge of one of the bookends, and place one of the silhouettes against it. Hold in place until the glue begins to set. Repeat with the second bookend and silhouette. Allow to fully dry before placing on your bookshelf.

step 11

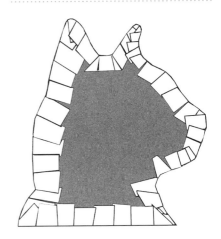

step 12

tray

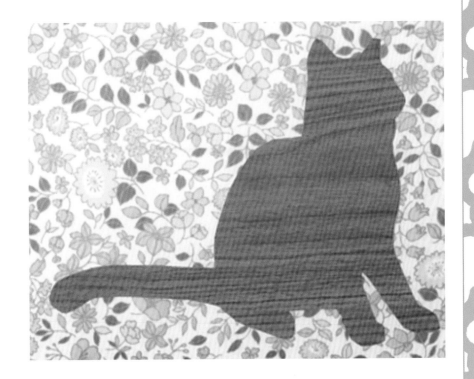

Trays are multifunctional, collecting our everyday objects, as well as serving refreshments to our friends and family. This simplified form of découpage is a fun and easy way to spruce up a tray without making a permanent commitment. Shelf-lining paper with adhesive is easy to cut and apply (and remove!), and comes in an endless amount of colors and styles. I used a wood-grain pattern for these projects, but that's just the tip of the iceberg.

difficulty:

1. If using one of the templates provided on pages 85–86, copy or trace it, resize if necessary, and cut out. If using your own image, enlarge or minimize it, print, and cut out.

2. Secure your template on the right side of the shelf-lining paper with a small loop of tape, taking notice of placement. Note: Some patterns don't require special placement, but others may require a bit more consideration.

3. Use the X-acto knife on a self-healing mat to cut carefully around the template. Remove the template.

4. Before adhering the shelf-lining paper, play around with placement on your tray.

5. Once you have desired placement, peel the backing off the paper and adhere to the tray, pressing firmly to smooth out air bubbles or other inconsistencies.

what else?

Choose the chalkboard variety of shelf-lining paper to make fun labels for a cheeseboard.

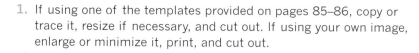

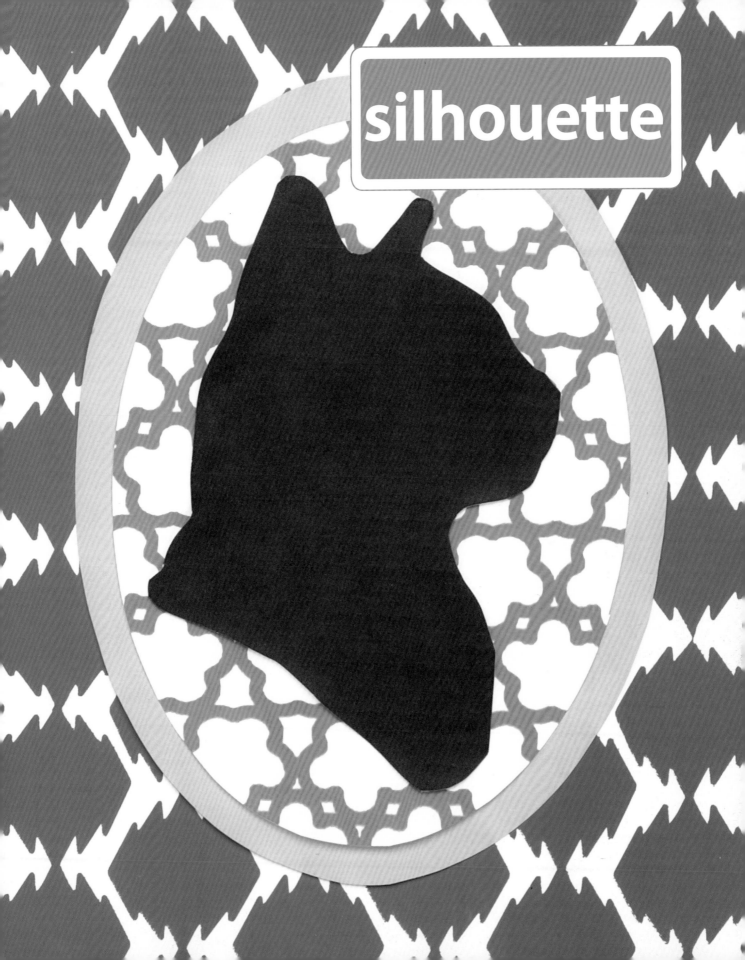

silhouette

materials

- 8" x 10" (20 x 25 cm) frame
- Silhouette template(s), page 86, or your own image
- Paper
- Ruler
- Pencil
- Scissors
- Construction paper, cardstock, or decorative paper
- X-acto knife
- Self-healing mat
- Craft glue
- Flat paintbrush

Victorian silhouettes are classic and modern, and the simplicity of the form allows for endless personalization. You can choose to exercise restraint by creating a black and white silhouette or give it a twist by introducing color and pattern. Consider scale, too: a larger piece can be commanding, while a smaller silhouette can be a sweet tribute to a best friend. Whatever your choice, you will, no doubt, end up with a unique artwork that complements any décor.

difficulty:

1. If not using an 8" x 10" (20 x 25 cm) frame, measure your frame's dimensions (length and width). This is an important step, as it will determine the size of your silhouette and any other elements you want to include.

2. Decide how you would like the silhouette to look. Do you want to keep it simple with just a silhouette on a uniform background or would you like to include the ovals to create depth and a bit more visual interest?

3. If you would like to include the ovals, copy or trace the large oval template provided on page 86, resize if necessary, and cut out. Note: You will want the larger oval to sit within the frame, not against the edges. Copy or trace the small oval template provided on page 86, resize if necessary—approximately 20 percent smaller than the large oval—and cut out. Set the ovals aside.

4. If using the silhouette template provided on page 86, copy or trace it, resize if necessary, and cut out. If using your own image, enlarge or minimize it, print, and cut out. Note: If including the oval templates, take note of the height of the smallest oval and size the silhouette to fit within the edges.

5. Trace the silhouette and ovals on the backside of the construction paper, cardstock, or decorative paper. Remove the templates. Use the X-acto knife on a self-healing mat to cut along the traced lines. Note: You are tracing on the backside of the paper, so if some of the traced lines remain after cutting, don't worry. They will be on the "wrong side" of the paper.

6. For the background paper, use the frame's glass as a template. Place the glass on the front side of the paper, hold steady with one hand, and cut around the glass with an X-acto knife. This assures that you get a perfect fit *(see illustration)*. Note: If you are using decorative paper, certain patterns may require a bit more consideration to assure visual balance within the frame.

step 6

what else?

For a quirky variation, use the Stamp template on page 87 in place of the traditional silhouette template. Copy or trace it, resize if necessary, and cut out.

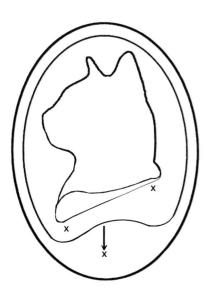

step 7

7. Place cut pieces on the background paper before gluing. Once you are satisfied with placement, gently lift the edge of each piece and make a faint pencil mark on the layer beneath. This is a registration mark that will guide you when gluing the pieces. Note: I like to make registration marks at the two bottom corners of the silhouette and the bottom center points of the ovals *(see illustration)*.

8. To adhere to the background paper, use the paintbrush to apply a thin, even layer of glue to the large oval or silhouette, depending on your design. Note: An even layer of glue is important because, depending on the weight of your paper, beads of glue may cause inconsistency on the surface. Align with registration mark(s) and apply to paper. Press firmly with clean hands, making sure to smooth out air bubbles or other inconsistencies. Continue gluing remaining elements, if necessary. Allow to dry, then frame and hang on your wall.

shade

materials

- Craft paper roll
- Smooth lamp shade, coolie or drum *(see illustration, opposite)*
- Pencil
- Straight-edge ruler
- Scissors
- Shade template(s), page 85, or your own image
- Paper
- Tape (transparent or masking)
- Paper clips
- Pushpin or nail
- Foam pad
- Craft glue
- Bias tape or ribbon
- Double-sided tape

While I like a pop of color or an interesting texture to enliven a design scheme, too much of a good thing can take elegance to gaudy in a single move. Often it's the small details that make a room special, and I think this shade really delivers in that way. It is customizable—you may choose to use different silhouettes for a varied appearance or create a repeat pattern using the same form. I chose to use natural-colored craft paper, not only because the tan hue softens the light but also because the contrast allows the perforations to appear crisp. The beauty of a perforated lampshade is that the design remains understated until you illuminate the lamp, then your handiwork takes center stage. Win, win.

difficulty:

1. Roll out the craft paper on a flat surface. Note: If you don't have a large table, the floor works just as well. Hold the lampshade so that its side is against the flat surface. Roll the lampshade to be sure that the placement enables you to complete one rotation while still on the paper.

2. Align your pencil with the seam at the top of the shade. Roll the shade and trace until it completes a full rotation *(see illustration)*. Continue tracing 1" (2.5 cm) beyond the seam to create an overlap. Note: Depending on the shape of your lampshade, this will either be a straight line (drum) or an arc (coolie).

3. Hold the shade in place and repeat step 2, tracing the bottom edge of the lampshade by rolling it in the reverse direction *(see illustration)*.

4. Using the straight-edge ruler and your pencil, connect the upper and lower lines at each end *(see illustration)*

5. Cut along the traced lines, as well as your lines from step 4. You now have a craft paper shade. Wrap the paper around the lampshade to ensure that it fits properly.

6. Lay the craft paper shade flat and measure the distance between the bottom and top edges. This measurement will give you a sense of your scale limitations. Play around with different silhouette sizes. If using one of the templates provided on page 85, copy or trace it, resize if necessary, and cut out. If using your own photograph, enlarge or minimize it, print, and cut out. Avoid placing your images within ½" (13 mm) of the ends, as this is will be where the the paper overlaps.

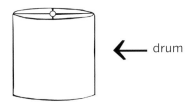
← drum

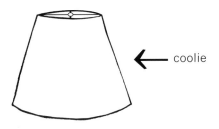
← coolie

materials

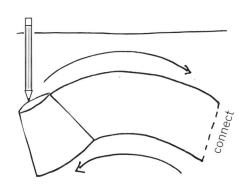

connect

steps 2–4

what else?

For a more permanent option, perforate a fabric lampshade. Simply position the stencil directly on the lampshade and use the pushpin or nail to create your design. When you are done, remove the stencil, re-place the shade, and turn on the lamp.

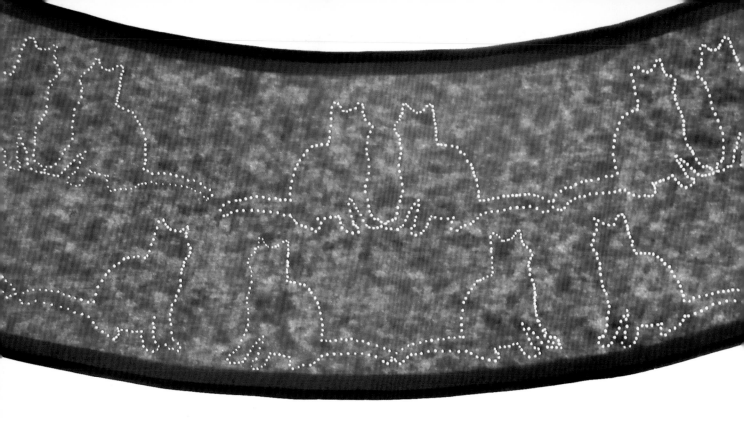

7. Once you decide on the pattern, copy or trace enough images to complete your design. Note: Do not cut the images along the outlines of the cats. Leave extra paper around the images. Lay them out on the craft paper and tape together, creating a stencil. Note: Do not tape the images directly to the craft paper. Use paper clips to secure the final design to the craft paper shade *(see illustration)*.

8. Lay the area of the craft paper that you want to punch on the foam pad and place your stencil on top of it. Using the pushpin or nail, punch through the stencil paper and craft paper, following the line of the image. Note: Try to create a rhythm with the holes, punching closely in an equidistant manner. Continue to punch until all of the images in your design have been perforated. Remove the stencil.

9. Wrap the craft paper around the lampshade. Use a small loop of tape, inside the overlap, to temporarily secure the shade. Turn on the lamp to see your handiwork.

10. Unwrap the shade and lay it on a flat surface. Apply a thin bead of glue along the top edge of the shade. With clean hands, begin at one end and apply the ribbon (drum) or bias tape (drum or coolie) to the shade. Note: If applying the bias tape use the fold of the tape to cover the paper's edge. If using ribbon, place it so the edge is slightly higher than the paper's edge to conceal the top of the shade. Extend the tape or ribbon ¾" (2 cm) beyond the shade's edge and cut. Repeat for the bottom edge of the shade. Allow to dry.

11. Wrap the craft paper shade around your lampshade, using a strip of double-sided tape to secure the overlap of both the paper and the trim.

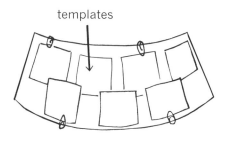

templates

step 7

to: rabbit from: Pony

materials

- Paper or fabric*, plus a little extra for test printing
- Stamp template, page 87, or your own image
- Paper
- Clear Plexiglas*
- Self-adhesive craft foam
- Tape (transparent or masking)
- Pencil
- X-acto knife
- Self-healing mat
- Palette knife
- Water-based ink
- Piece of glass with masking tape around the edges
- Soft brayer
- Paper towel or clean rag

See opposite page to learn more about these materials.

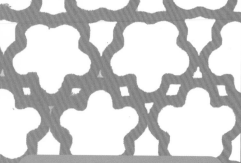

Making a handmade stamp for fabric or paper can be rewarding and fun because it is reusable and almost limitless in its application. Whether you want to create your own fabric, decorate an existing garment or accessory, or make custom wrapping paper, one stamp can do it all. The most important thing to remember when printing by hand is that the irregularities are what make the print unique. While the consistency in other forms of printing has its merits, it is the evidence of the hand that makes stamping so special. Once you get the hang of stamping, apply your newfound skill to the Placemat project on page 76.

difficulty:

WORKING WITH THE MATERIALS

PLEXIGLAS

Clear Plexiglas makes a great base for the stamp because it is non-porous, uniform, and transparent. Sometimes, when stamping, you will make a print but not be completely satisfied with the ink coverage. Plexiglas allows you to make a second pass at the print because you are able to see the area and realign the stamp. I don't recommend this for every pass of the stamp (after all, it's the irregularity of the stamp that makes it unique), but, certainly, if you feel you would like more coverage, the transparency of Plexiglas makes it possible.

FABRIC

Preparation: It is always best to read the instructions for materials you are using, as different formulas may require different treatments. For printing on fabric, purchase water-based ink specifically formulated for this application. Always wash fabric before printing because fabric softeners or other additives will inhibit the absorption of ink.

Printing: When printing on fabric, you are essentially staining the material, so it's necessary to give some time for the pigment to absorb. Apply consistent, even pressure to the stamp for a count of twenty to insure that the fabric accepts the ink. You may find that using a secondary object, in conjunction with your body weight, will yield the intended result. Try something heavy and flat, like a book (covered to protect the jacket) or a brick, to help get the consistent pressure you desire.

Heat-setting: Once the ink is dry, it is necessary to heat-set the print before laundering. Water-based fabric ink requires heat-setting because the heat activates the pigment. Even when the ink is completely air-dried, it still retains a small amount of water. Applying a hot iron to the print will render the ink permanent. A household iron, on the highest setting for the fabric that you are using, will do the trick. You can test the ink by rubbing a small area with a wet fingertip. If it feels gummy, then it is not set properly.

PAPER

There are many different types of paper and each one has its own relationship with ink. Some papers are coated, allowing the ink to sit on top of the surface, while others are created specifically for wet media, allowing the ink to absorb into the fibers. Testing the paper first will give you a sense of what you are working with, yielding more successful results. Through trial and error, you will learn how much ink and pressure to apply to any given surface. Remember, perfection isn't the goal here; the evidence of the hand is what we're looking for when using the stamping method.

MAKING THE STAMP

1. If printing fabric, prepare it by laundering and pressing. Set aside.

2. If using the template provided on page 87, copy or trace it, resize if necessary, and cut out. If using your own image, enlarge or minimize it, print, and cut out. Note: Avoid using an image with too much detail, as the detail can get lost in the printing process. Also, the image will stamp in reverse.

3. Choose a piece of Plexiglas that is slightly larger than your cutout image.

4. Adhere your image to the self-adhesive craft foam with a loop of tape and trace. Remove the template.

5. Using the X-acto knife, follow the traced lines, cutting through the foam, into the desired shape.

6. Remove the backing from the foam and adhere to the center of the piece of Plexiglas. Press firmly and hold to assure that it is secure.

PRINTING

7. Prepare the surface to be printed: lay your paper or fabric flat, with ample room around you to maneuver and set up the printing materials.

8. Use the palette knife to retrieve a tablespoon-sized (15 ml) dollop of ink and place it in the center of the piece of glass. Roll the brayer back and forth through the ink until you achieve an even coating on the brayer.

9. Place the stamp, foam side up, on a flat surface. Stabilize the stamp with one hand, then roll the brayer over the foam several times until the foam is coated evenly. Note: Before printing, check to make sure that the Plexiglas around the foam is free of rogue ink. Use the paper towel or clean rag to remove excess ink.

10. Make a test stamp on the extra material that you set aside. Note: This is a necessary step as it enables you to troubleshoot before you commit to printing your project. You may discover that you've put too much ink on the stamp or not enough. Or you may choose to tweak the design a bit.

11. Print by placing the inked side of the stamp against the material. Apply direct pressure across the entire stamp by placing your palm across the back of the stamp and leaning in with your body weight. Note: Stamps vary in size, so use your judgment and apply pressure as needed. If the stamp is larger than your palm, be sure to apply pressure to all areas while it is in contact with the material. Different materials require various levels of pressure and time in contact with the stamp. Please refer to page 73 for specific instructions by material.

12. Once you are satisfied with the stamp quality, it's time to start printing. Repeat steps 9 and 11. Note: When printing on fabric, it is necessary to re-ink the stamp after every print. Paper is less absorbent so you may be able to re–ink every other print or so. Also, with paper, the time in contact with the stamp is significantly less, so make sure to do a test to familiarize yourself with the material.

what else?

You can choose to map your design out in advance or print freestyle for a more organic feel. No matter which approach you choose, the result will be unique and one of a kind.

placemat

A placemat for your little buddy says, "Nobody should eat (directly) off the floor." Cotton duck is a naturally water-resistant material that is well suited for a pet's placemat. It's washable but can also withstand less than perfect table manners without having to be regularly laundered.

difficulty:

1. Prepare fabric by laundering and pressing. Print fabric with the stamp and heat-set.

2. Measure and cut a 13" x 19" (33 x 48 cm) piece of fabric.

3. Beginning on one of the short sides, make ½" (13 mm) fold. Pin to secure (optional). Iron fold to create a crisp edge, removing pins as you go. Repeat with the other short side.

4. Repeat step 3 on each of the long sides.

5. Fold and press both of the short sides again, ½" (13 mm), pinning as you go.

6. Repeat step 5 with the long sides.

7. Using your sewing machine, stitch ¼" (6 mm) from the edge. Start at one corner and proceed around the perimeter of the placemat, pivoting around the corners, until you are back where you started.

materials

- ½ yd (46 cm) fabric (cotton duck or canvas)
- Palette knife
- Water-based ink
- Piece of glass with masking tape around the edges
- Soft brayer
- Stamp
- Paper towel or clean rag
- Iron
- Ruler
- Fabric shears
- Pins
- Thread
- Sewing machine

what else?

Add a decorative edge to your pet placemat by stitching rickrack or another fun trim onto it after it is sewn.

friend

materials

- ½ yd (46 cm) lightweight fabric
- Friend templates, page 87
- Fabric shears
- Pins
- Tailor's pencil or chalk
- Thread
- Sewing machine
- Point turner
- Fill
- Hand-sewing needle
- 3 buttons (2 eyes, 1 nose)
- Embroidery thread, in a contrasting color

A handmade kitty friend is a great gift for adults and children alike. Or make one for yourself—you deserve it! The simple design combined with your choice of fabric and buttons will create a kitty full of personality and style. Sprinkle the fill with lavender for a cute, relaxing, and fragrant bed buddy.

difficulty:

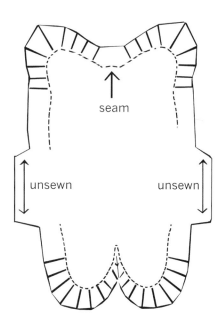

seam

unsewn   unsewn

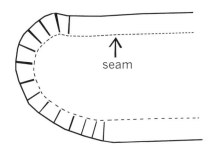

seam

step 7

1. Prepare fabric by laundering and pressing.

2. Copy or trace the templates provided on page 87, enlarge 200 percent, and cut out. Set aside.

3. Cut two 12" x 12" (30 x 30 cm) pieces of fabric and place right sides together. Pin.

4. Place the templates on the fabric, with at least 2" (5 cm) between them, taking notice of the fabric's pattern to be sure that you like the direction of the print. Note: You need to cut two arms.

5. Trace the solid lines of the templates using the tailor's pencil. Note: The dotted lines designate the areas that are to be left unsewn. Remove the templates.

6. Stitch along the traced lines with the sewing machine.

7. Trim the fabric ¼" (6 mm) from the seams of the three sewn pieces (body and two arms). Snip the areas where the seams curve, at a perpendicular angle to the seams *(see illustration)*. Be careful not to clip the seams. Note: Notching the fabric in this way will encourage the shape of the curves when the fabric is inverted in the next step.

what else?

This project is a great party activity for older children. Sew the body and arm pieces in advance, and let them stuff, attach the arms, and decorate their own kitties with a selection of buttons.

8. Invert the fabric of all three pieces, using a point turner to encourage the inversion of the seams. Note: Invert the body through one of the armholes.

9. Stuff the body and arms, using the point turner or your hand to encourage the fill into the three pieces until they are sufficiently full.

10. Tuck in the excess fabric ¼" (6 mm) at one of the the armholes. Position one of the arms with a third of its length inside the body. Hand-sew by starting inside the body, just above the arm, and passing the needle back and forth, from front to back, until secure *(see illustration)*. Tie the thread off. Repeat with the other armhole and arm.

11. Place the buttons on the face. Note: Play around with different widths between the eyes to give your kitty some added character.

12. Once you have desired button placement, use embroidery thread to sew the buttons in place. To sew each button, begin by passing the needle through the fabric first. This will conceal the thread behind the button once it's attached. When done sewing each button, tie the thread off.

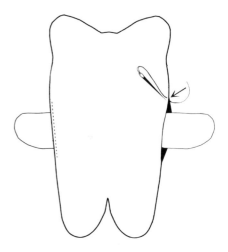

step 10

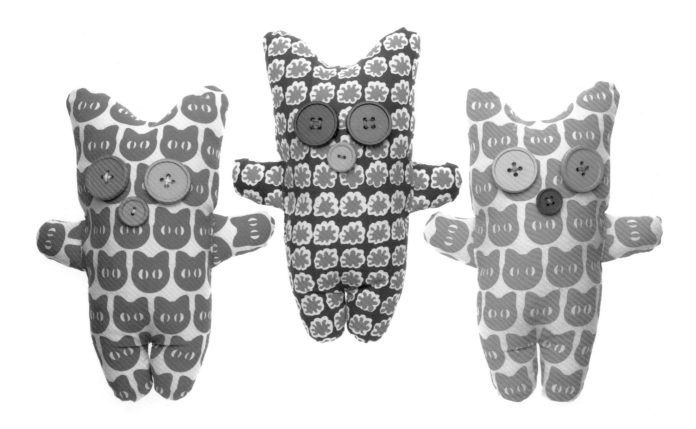

templates

MOUSE (page 16)

FISH (page 33)

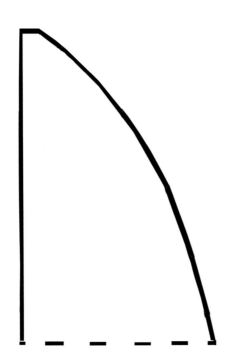

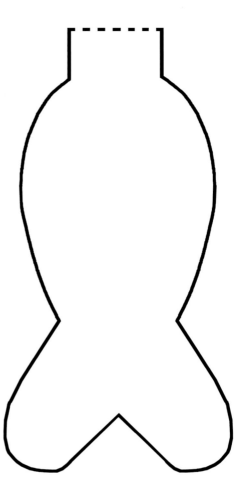

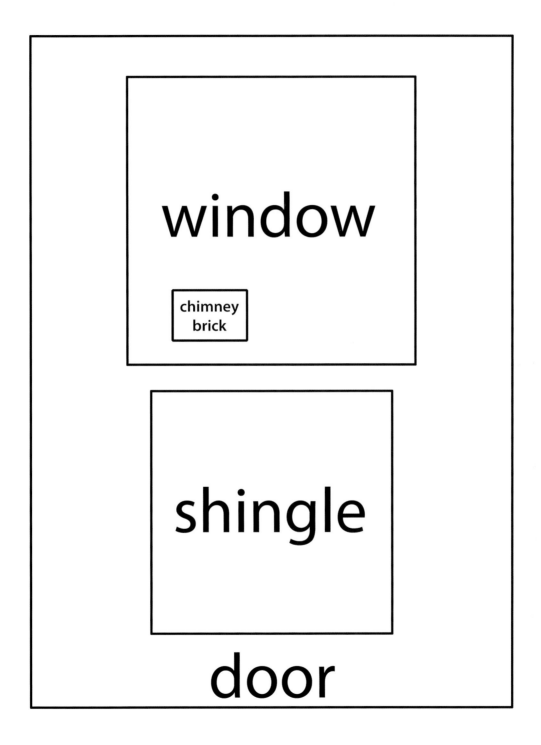

window

chimney
brick

shingle

door

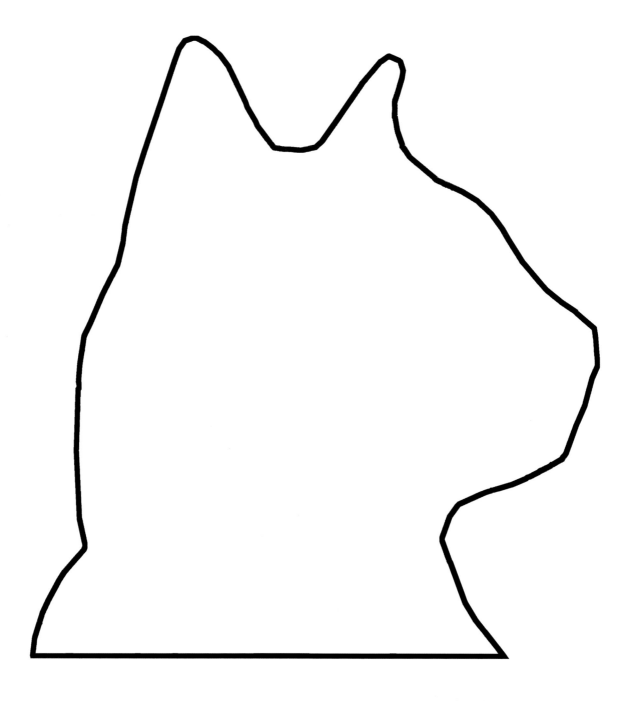

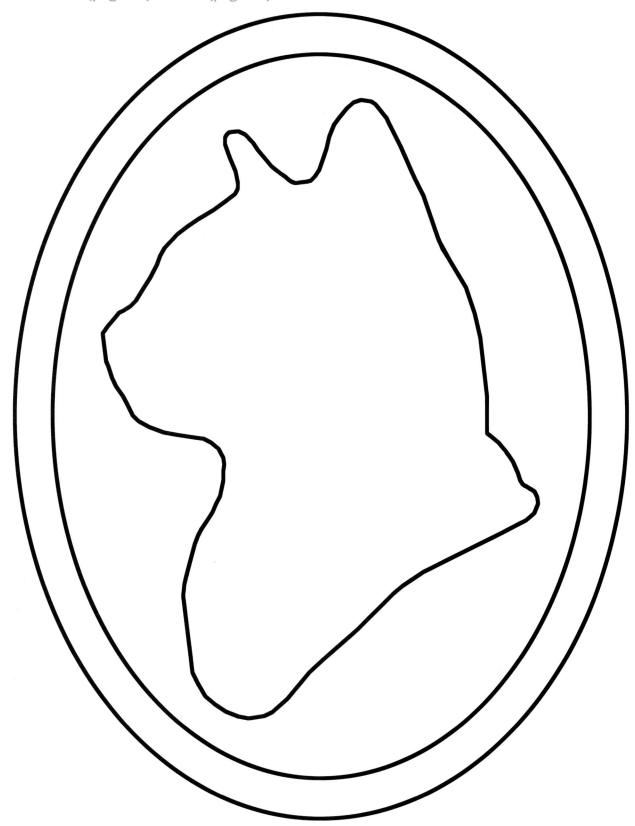

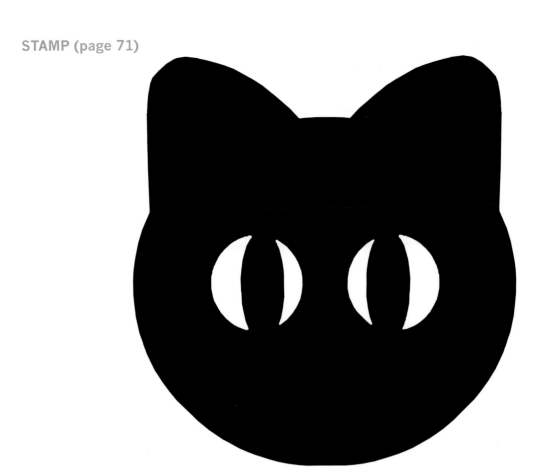

FRIEND (page 78)
enlarge 200 percent

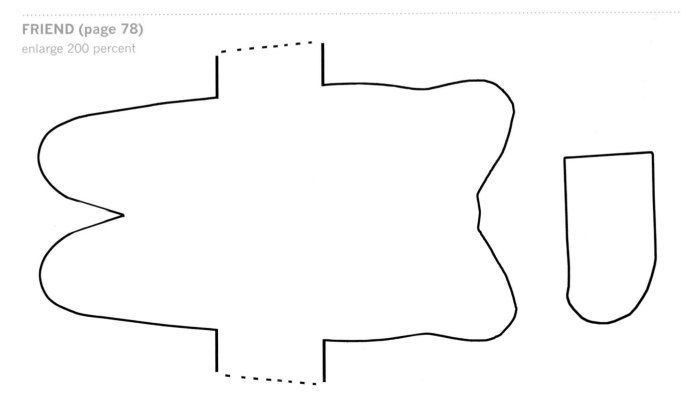

materials glossary

ACRYLIC CRAFT PAINT available at art and craft stores.

ADHESIVE SHELF-LINING PAPER usually comes in a roll. Available at hardware and home improvement stores.

BATTING (cotton, wool, or polyester) 100-percent cotton batting is the most breathable and is available in most craft and fabric outlets and online. Wool batting, another natural option, is very warm, but it can be costly and more difficult to locate. Polyester batting is the most widely available and the least expensive. It's the least breathable but is available in a wide range of lofts (thicknesses), making it a more accommodating option.

BIAS TAPE a narrow strip of fabric, cut on the bias, which enables it to be more fluid and great for finishing edges. Available in many colors at fabric and sewing notions retailers, or you can make your own.

BUTTONS come in a variety of shapes, sizes, and materials. Available at craft, fabric, and sewing notions retailers.

CAN (empty) any size works. (I reused a coffee can for the Grass project on page 19.)

CARDBOARD BOX try to reuse boxes when you can, except for the House project on page 49, which requires new boxes for best results. Available at office supply retailers, paper suppliers, and shipping centers.

CARDBOARD TUBE (heavy duty) often available, for free, at carpet retailers. Call ahead and ask if they have one available. The tube may need to be cut to a smaller length—inquire if the carpet store will cut it or use a utility knife to carefully cut to desired length.

CARDSTOCK a heavier paper. Available at art and craft stores, paper product suppliers, and office supply retailers.

CATNIP available in its dried form at pet stores.

CHARCOAL formulated for container gardening. Available at garden centers, nurseries, home improvement centers, and aquarium stores.

CLOTHESLINE braided, cotton rope. Available at hardware stores and home improvement retailers.

CONSTRUCTION PAPER for the House project on page 49, use the archival kind to prevent fading. Available at art and craft stores, paper product suppliers, and office supply retailers.

COPY PAPER (8½" x 14", or 21.5 x 35.5 cm) also know as legal size paper. For the Star project on page 41, choose a vibrant color, such as yellow. Available at office supply stores.

COTTON DUCK (or CANVAS) a heavyweight, plain, woven cotton fabric. Available at fabric stores.

CRAFT GLUE (or ALL-PURPOSE GLUE) choose a non-toxic version. Available at art, craft, and hardware stores.

CRAFT PAPER ROLL (natural color) available at office supply retailiers, art and craft stores, and paper suppliers.

DECORATIVE PAPER available at craft stores and paper product suppliers. (You may also choose to make your own decorative paper with the Stamp project on page 71.)

DOWEL ROD available at hardware and home improvement stores.

EMBROIDERY THREAD a thin yarn used in embroidery and needlework projects. Available at craft, fabric, and sewing notions retailers.

FABRIC for the projects in this book, use a lightweight, durable, 100-percent cotton fabric, such as poplin, unless directed otherwise. Available at fabric stores and some craft outlets.

FABRIC INK (water-based) specially formulated for use on fabric, but also suitable for application on paper. Available at art and craft stores.

FABRIC SHEARS scissors for cutting only fabric. Available at craft, fabric, and sewing notions retailers.

FILL (wool, cotton, or polyester) any of these types of fill can be used in the projects requiring a little extra cushion. See **BATTING** for detailed characteristics of each type of material.

FOAM for the Ball project on page 29 and the Shade project on page 67, look for a foam pad that is at least a few inches (7.5 cm) thick, and dense in texture. Available at craft stores and stores specializing in yarn. For the Bed project on page 26, you will need foam that is sold by the yard (meter). Available in craft and fabric stores.

FRAME choose an 8" x 10" (20 x 25 cm) frame for the Silhouette project on page 63, as the template provided is sized to this scale. Available in art, craft, and home stores.

GARDEN STONES (small) available at garden centers, nurseries, and home improvement centers

GLASS (with masking tape around the edges) enables easy application and clean-up of ink for the Stamp project on page 71. (The masking tape protects you from any sharp edges.) Reuse a piece of glass from a small window or frame. See also **PLEXIGLAS**.

GRASS SEEDS (wheat grass or rye) available at garden centers, nurseries, and home improvement centers.

GROSGRAIN RIBBON a classic style of ribbon characterized by its graphic stripe and ribbed texture that comes in a variety of colors and widths. Available at craft, fabric, and sewing notions retailers.

HAND-SEWING NEEDLE often comes in a multisize pack. Choose a needle that suits the fabric you are using: the higher the needle number, the lighter the fabric it sews. Available at craft, fabric, and sewing notions retailers.

HOT GLUE GUN (and GLUE STICKS) a glue that dries quickly and is great for large-scale projects. Available at craft stores.

IRON (and IRONING BOARD) necessary for projects that utilize fabric.

JAR (clear) any size will work. (I reused a small yogurt jar, among others, for the Grass project on page 19.)

JINGLE BELL available at craft stores.

JUTE CORD a natural rope with a scratchy texture. Available at hardware and craft stores

LAMPSHADE choose a smooth one in a coolie or drum shape. Available at craft, fabric, and sewing notions retailers.

LAUNDRY DETERGENT (unscented) available at grocery stores.

LEATHER CORD (thin) often sold by the yard (meter). Available at craft stores.

METAL BOOKEND comes in a variety of sizes. Choose a size appropriate for the heft of the books that you would like to display. (I chose a pair that are 5", or 12.5 cm, tall.) Available at office supply stores and retailers that provide organizational products.

NAIL (and HAMMER) for the Grass project on page 19, any size will work. For the Shade project on page 67, nail size will depend on type of perforation you prefer.

NEEDLE-FELTING TOOL a thin and extremely sharp barbed needle used to pierce wool roving to produce a knitted effect, rendering the wool into felt. Available at craft stores and some stores specializing in yarn.

PAINTBRUSH (flat) A flat brush is made with the fibers aligned in a row, creating a flat, uniform edge, and comes in variety of sizes and quality. Choose an acrylic craft brush, measuring approximately 1" (2.5 cm) in width. Available at art and craft stores.

PALETTE KNIFE a blunt tool used for mixing and applying ink or paint. Available at art stores.

PAPER any type of paper can be used for copying or tracing templates. Available at office supply stores and paper product suppliers.

PAPER TAPE a specialty packing tape made of paper, with a strong adhesive applied to one side. Available at office supply stores and paper product suppliers.

PINKING SHEARS the sawtooth blade prevents edges of cut fabric from unraveling. Available at craft, fabric, and sewing notions retailers.

PINS choose long straight pins for holding fabric in place. Available at craft, fabric, and sewing notions retailers.

PLASTIC WRAP choose the type used in food storage and preparation. Available at grocery stores.

PLEXIGLAS (clear) this unbreakable alternative to glass comes in a range of thicknesses. Available at hardware stores and online.

POINT TURNER a wooden sewing tool for inverting fabric and pushing out corners. (You can also use a chopstick, the end of a paintbrush, or the non-writing end of a pen.) Available at craft, fabric, and sewing notions retailers.

POLYURETHANE (water-based) a non-toxic sealant that protects acrylic paint and provides a gloss finish. Available at art, craft, and hardware stores.

POTTING SOIL available at garden centers, nurseries, and home improvement stores.

PUSHPIN available at office supply and home improvement stores.

PVC PIPE comes in a variety of lengths, and, depending on the retailer, may also be cut to size. Available at home improvement stores.

RIBBON for the Shade project on page 67, the ribbon is decorative, so choose a style, color, and width based on your personal preference and/or design scheme. Available at craft, fabric, and sewing notions retailers.

RICKRACK a zigzaggy trim often sold by the yard (meter). Available at craft, fabric, and sewing notions retailers.

SAND PAPER (fine grain) available at hardware and home improvement stores.

SCISSORS a basic pair for cutting paper.

SELF-ADHESIVE CRAFT FOAM a sheet of thin foam treated with an adhesive on one side that is an excellent material to use in the creation of custom stamps. It cuts easily and adheres to Plexiglas. Available at art and craft stores.

SELF-HEALING MAT designed to withstand the sharp edge of X-acto knives and other tools that require precision cutting on a flat surface, while protecting the surface of your table or counter. (You can use a spare piece of cardboard or foamcore in its place, but neither is as friendly to the X-acto blade.) Available at art and craft stores.

SEWING MACHINE a basic machine. (For these projects, you only need to use a straight stitch and reverse stitch.)

SEWABLE VELCRO STRIP available at fabric and sewing notions retailers.

SISAL ROPE (twisted) available in the rope department of hardware stores and home improvement centers.

SOFT BRAYER used in the printing process to apply a uniform coat of ink to a stamp or printing block. Available at art and craft stores.

STRAIGHT-EDGE RULER a stainless steel ruler used for drawing and cutting straight lines. Available at art and craft stores.

TAILOR'S PENCIL (or CHALK) a tool used to mark fabric that can be brushed off easily. Choose a color that will be visible on your fabric. Available at fabric and sewing notions retailers.

THREAD 100-percent cotton all-purpose thread is best for the projects in this book. Choose a color that matches the dominant color of your fabric, or one that is a shade lighter. You may also choose to use a complementary color. Available at craft, fabric, and sewing notions retailers.

TRAY wood, metal, or plastic of any size. Available at home stores.

WOODEN DISC available at hardware stores in the decorative wood section. (I purchased the wooden disc for the Scratch Post project on page 45 at Lowe's.)

WOOL ROVING carded, unspun wool that is suitable for spinning and felting. Available at craft and yarn stores and online.

X-ACTO KNIFE a very sharp blade used for precision cutting. When buying an X-acto knife, purchase some extra blades (sold separately), as they tend to lose their effectiveness with use and will need to be replaced. Available at art and craft stores.

resources

ART SUPPLIES

BLICK ART MATERIALS
dickblick.com

HOBBY LOBBY
hobbylobby.com

MICHAELS CRAFT STORES
michaels.com

NEW YORK CENTRAL ART SUPPLY
nycentralart.com

FABRIC

B&J FABRICS
bandjfabrics.com

FABRICWORM
fabricworm.com

JO-ANN FABRIC AND CRAFT STORES
joann.com

NEW YORK ELEGANT FABRICS
nyelegantfabrics.com

PURL SOHO
purlsoho.com

GARDEN SUPPLIES

CHELSEA GARDEN CENTER
chelseagardencenter.com

HOME DEPOT
homedepot.com

KEIL BROS
keilbros.net

LOWE'S HOME IMPROVEMENT
lowes.com

HARDWARE

GARBER HARDWARE
garberhardware.com

HOME DEPOT
homedepot.com

LOWE'S HOME IMPROVEMENT
lowes.com

PAPER PRODUCTS

KATE'S PAPERIE
katespaperie.com

PAPER MART
papermart.com

ULINE
uline.com

PLEXIGLAS

CANAL PLASTICS CENTER
canalplastic.com

SEWING SUPPLIES AND NOTIONS

DAYTONA TRIMMING
daytonatrim.com

HOBBY LOBBY
hobbylobby.com

JO-ANN FABRIC AND CRAFT STORES
joann.com

MICHAELS CRAFT STORES
michaels.com

SIL THREAD
silthreadinc.com

WOOL ROVING

BROOKLYN GENERAL
brooklyngeneral.com

HOBBY LOBBY
hobbylobby.com

MICHAELS CRAFT STORES
michaels.com

THE YARN TREE
theyarntree.com

index

It would be ridiculous to take credit for a book when there were so many people who provided me with emotional, technical, and creative support along the way. Thank you to the talented and clever Erin Canning for providing the vision for this project and to One Peace Books for giving me the opportunity to make it a reality.

Thank you to my Grandparents, Milton G. Hulme and Helen Cloherty Hulme, for their deep generosity and love.

A giant thank you to Alyson Baker and Zach Hadlock for allowing me to photograph in their beautiful home. Thanks also to Platform FAF for the use of their exquisite furniture and wood bowls.

Every creative person needs a friend like Jen MacDonald. We came up with the idea for kitty jones together, and she's been immensely supportive of it ever since. Thank you for being a sounding board and making me laugh.

Thank you to Mark Gagnon, a wildly imaginative and talented artist, whose work ethic is unmatched and whose early support for kitty jones sustained my resolve when I questioned my direction. You have been a great friend to me.

This book would never have come together without the book design by Nancy Leonard and the photography of Mark Gore. Nancy's talent and professional manner calmed my nerves in uncertain times. The memory of Mark's laidback style and welcoming attitude toward the rotation of cats in his studio will make me smile for years to come. And also a big thanks to our top model, Vivian.

My Mother and her dear friend, Joan Dickey Shanahan, are largely responsible for fostering my early creativity. One time, when I was dissatisfied with one of my drawings, Mrs, Shanahan explained to me that I was frustrated because the drawing wasn't finished yet. That advice is something that I have carried with me and is as valuable in my creative process as it is in my daily life. Thanks, Aunt Joan.

To my dearest friends, Shawn Coker Smith, Jocelyn Shoup, Courtney Higham, Catherine Higham, Valerie Nolan, Sarah Hegarty, Sarah Reisman, Paulina Berczynski, Denise Shanahan, Melissa Gregory Rue, and Jemima Farwell: You have all supported me and inspired me in ways that are far too vast to explain here. I appreciate you all so much and am grateful for your friendship.

Thank you to the Salty Paw, my first store: You've been with me since the beginning, and I will never forget it.

And lastly, thank you to Lucy and Peachbunny: For everything.

about the cats

rabbit

pony

Peachbunny was found in the hall on a cold night in January 2008. He enjoys making biscuits, pushing things off countertops. and playing fetch. A few times a year he travels to Pennsylvania to visit his Grandparents and Uncle Oliver the Golden Retriever. He likes to watch nature videos in his spare time.

Pony and Rabbit were born in 2000 in a junkyard in Brooklyn, New York. Here they were weaned on baked ziti until they tricked two humans into taking them into their home. Now they live in Queens, where Rabbit wishes he and Pony were best friends, and Pony wishes he was an only child.

Slushie, once sleek and streetwise, is now a twelve-year-old less sleek and extremely domestic cat living with three humans, one very large dog, one very small hamster, six snails, and a giant frog in Brooklyn, New York.